# A POEM A DAY
# A THANK YOU COLLECTION:

by Fran Bridger

Published by Exmoor News

Copyright © 2020 Fran Bridger

All rights reserved, no part of this publication may be reproduced, stored in a retrieval system, or transmitted in any form or by any means, electronic or mechanical, by photocopying, recording or otherwise, without prior permission in writing from the author.

ISBN - 978-1-9162718-3-8

# A POEM A DAY

# A THANK YOU COLLECTION:

### FOR MARIE CURIE: APRIL – MAY 2020

Welcome to my collection of poems written in order to raise funds for the Marie Curie Charity.

In April 2020, during the Covid 19 outbreak, all charities had been forced to close, and yet many charities such as Marie Curie, were having to work harder and longer than ever before, and often in unsafe conditions. At that time I had had experience of the kindness and the wonderful support afforded by Marie Curie and decided to write A Poem A Day to help them.

This is a collection of humour, serious, spiritual and lyrical poems, and I hope there are many that you like. They chart the beginning of my challenge, the march of the Covid 19 virus and how people were responding to it, they chart the bursting forth of Spring in the blossom of the cherry trees and the first-born lambs. Then as the days and weeks pass the poems reflect how people's thoughts turn to freedom, getting out and about, what they are missing most, and at that time how the fleece on the sheep grow hot in the warm Spring sunshine. There are poems of humour and poems of faith, and through it all I hope that there are many poems that you like, even those dealing with the burgeoning sense of loss of family, idleness, boredom, and longings to meet up etc.

We live in a fortunate part of the world and even though the Covid outbreak has taken away 'things' that we thought were of value it has also given us a new sense of value of the things that are important to us. We have come to value our homes, our gardens, our families, we have come to regret the loss of the freedom to have coffee with our friends, to go shopping, to go out when we feel like it, simply because we can. But we have also grown to value the importance of the postman/lady, the refuse collectors, the delivery person, the shop staff, the care assistants, and many, many more. We have come to recognise that the staff of the NHS face germs every day, in unsafe conditions, and that their courage has never before been noticed.

We have a new sense of respect for everyone, and for nature, and I pray that this continues.


Fran Bridger

## ACKNOWLEDGEMENTS

I would like to thank my lovely husband Mac, for his support when I needed it in difficult times, and when deciding to write A Poem A Day for Marie Curie his encouragement. Thank you for laughing at the humorous poems and for being a true confidante and friend for the more gutty poems about Covid 19.

I would also like to thank the Bridport Writing Community Facebook for all their support when I was posting these poems online, and especially to Max who wrote my challenge into an article for their online news.

Finally, thank you to all those who have supported Marie Curie because of my poems.

Fran Bridger

# Contents

MORNING HAS BROKEN . . . . . . . . . . . . . . . . . . . . . . . 1

SPRING LAMBS . . . . . . . . . . . . . . . . . . . . . . . . . . . . 2

CHILDREN . . . . . . . . . . . . . . . . . . . . . . . . . . . . . . . 3

GOOD FRIDAY: CHERRY TREE AND TULIPS . . . . . . . . . . 4

EASTER SUN RISING . . . . . . . . . . . . . . . . . . . . . . . . 5

THE ZION TREE . . . . . . . . . . . . . . . . . . . . . . . . . . . 6

SUN-DAY . . . . . . . . . . . . . . . . . . . . . . . . . . . . . . . 8

FIGURES . . . . . . . . . . . . . . . . . . . . . . . . . . . . . . . . 9

USE OF A SYMBOL . . . . . . . . . . . . . . . . . . . . . . . . 11

FREEDOM . . . . . . . . . . . . . . . . . . . . . . . . . . . . . . 12

PETRIFIED AND MOVING ON . . . . . . . . . . . . . . . . . 13

THE SONG OF DAWN . . . . . . . . . . . . . . . . . . . . . . 14

HOLDING BREATH IN AWE OF BEAUTY . . . . . . . . . . . 15

THE GREAT ESCAPE . . . . . . . . . . . . . . . . . . . . . . . 16

| | |
|---|---|
| HECTOR COMES TO TEA | 18 |
| CAT NAP CHARADE | 20 |
| LONGINGS | 22 |
| WAR TIME POVERTY | 23 |
| NOW YOU SEE IT, NOW YOU DON'T | 24 |
| IT'S CLEANING TIME | 25 |
| HANKERIN' TO BE IDLE | 26 |
| HAIKU | 27 |
| WOOLLEN LIFE | 28 |
| FUTURE DREAR | 29 |
| LOST | 30 |
| THE VITAL DIFFERENCE | 31 |
| COVID 2020 | 33 |
| REDUNDANCIES | 35 |
| WHEN THIS VIRUS IS OVER | 38 |
| VE CELEBRATIONS | 40 |
| WHAT CAN YOU DO NOW? | 43 |

# INDEX

## Morning has broken
In praise of Marie Curie staff, and in response to the closure of churches

## Spring lambs
The first of the Spring poems - a bird's eye view from a window

## Children

## Good Friday: Cherry tree and tulips

## Easter Sun Rising
With 'lockdown' restrictions our usual Service at a memorial stone had been cancelled. This is based on memories

## The Zion Tree
An Alphabet acrostic poem

## Sun-day

## Figures
At this time Captain Tom Moore was well on the way to his 100th birthday, and to eventually raising over £34 million for NHS charities. Well done, Capt. Tom.

## Use of a symbol

**Freedom**
    Life for many revolved around the home and the garden because of the virus.

**Petrified and moving on**

**The song of dawn**

**Holding breath in awe of beauty**

**The great escape**
    A humorous poem – fiction and fact!

**Hector comes to tea**

**Cat Nap Charade**

**Longings**
    The virus restrictions could last for months.
    Loneliness set in for many grandparents and parents.

**War time poverty**
    Based upon Mum's tiny brass thimble, early 20$^{th}$ C.
    We are so fortunate today

**Now you see it, now you don't**
    Humour: missing the seaside

**It's cleaning time**
    Humour: Spring cleaning and gardening like never before

**Hankerin' to be idle**
   Humour

**HAIKU:**
   Two short poems in Japanese style to tickle the mind

**Woollen life**

**Future drear**

**Lost**
   Hope: A beacon shines for everyone

**The vital difference**
   Hope:

**Covid 2020**
   Looking ahead:

**Redundancies**
   Fact and appreciation

**When this virus is over**

**VE Celebrations**

## MORNING HAS BROKEN

This opening poem will be difficult for me

Expressing my gratitude to all at M. C.

    Their nurses were superb, it really must be said

    They washed and they turned, made him comfortable in bed;

They laughed and they chattered, and they made our Bob smile

They made us feel human and supported for a while;

    They came late, and early, and during the day

    It was amazing their presence kept sadness at bay.

The days turned to nights, and the nights turned to days

A special moment was hearing Bob sing Songs of Praise;

    *Morning has broken* has new meaning for me

    Since Bob is no longer here, only his memory.

The Virus came and restrictions were enforced

No funeral service, but a burial of course.

    No collections could be made for the amazing M. C.

    Which still does its work, so it's partly up to me

To raise some funds for a big Thank you

From a family you helped, a dream you made come true

    Please sponsor me to write a poem each day

    And a great big **Thank you** is all I can say!

# SPRING LAMBS

Spring

Shooting up buds and blossoms to new horizons

Lambs

Galloping and gambolling through newly grown grass;

Birds

Building basinettes in branches for their babies;

Hedgehogs

Hurrying through hedgerows finding homes for hoglets;

Primroses

Golden posies of some dew filled springtime flowers;

NHS

Nurses, carers, in danger everywhere.  Clappings.

## CHILDREN

Baa-ing,
    A sheep ambles across the land
    looking for her disconsolate lamb
that was crying in some field
    out of sight,
        All around her lambs raced
    twisting and high kicking
tails bouncing upon shoulders
    leaping upon the grass
        in the long spring time
    spreading thin days into summer.
Now tussling heads together
rubbing soft ears into a bunch of felted wool.
A woollen blanket.
    They were our children rough boxing,
throwing punches that never were meant to hurt
    laughing in the other's face
        chasing across the park
    youth pounding in footsteps.
Lambs and children bleating.

## GOOD FRIDAY: CHERRY TREE AND TULIPS

Buds are clinging to the cherry tree outside my window

Bursting from their winter shells at the swoop

Of the icy wind blowing from the north;

Bunches of flowers and buds of leaves cluster along the branches

While the tulips are rioting among the roses

Splashing scarlet and gold through my garden canvas

And here I am, creating Earth's eternal spring

In a mutiny of rebellious red

And pink cherry blossom.

This week the branches are full of chaos:

Buds jostling with petals;

Leaves intent on entering the world

Popping in a confusion of vermilion and lime

Likened to the chaos of heaven and thanksgiving

For another year lived through and waited upon

For this day,

This good day,

This black and white Friday.

## EASTER SUN RISING

*The walk is easy after the early call*
*of the scarce used alarm clock '5 bells and all*
*is well'. A cup of tea and energy bar*
*was all the food we could swallow before*
*we're off on our annual hike to the moors,*
*feeling the chill though still inspired of course*
*by birdsong and deer; trying to beat the sun*
*rising, and shouting 'I see its rays. Let's run'.*
*Noses assailed by the cinnamon perfume*
*Of gorse, golden in the morning's misted gloom;*
*Running to beat the sun rising in the east*
*and crying against a hint of cloud, our feast*
*bouncing upon my back, then seeing the crowd*
*expectant, already gathered at the Stone*
*worshipping God's rising, before going home.*

## THE ZION TREE

And did those feet in ancient time

Bend at the knee for want of rhyme;

Could poets dream or art

Devour the principals that

Each require to spread the word or

Feed each dream that each had heard for

Greater schemes and greater art

Here heralding each man his part

In making known how life is lived

Just proving that we can forgive.

Kind thoughts are best for words of prose

Like love, and nature, and to those

Most folk respond with smiles and cheer.

No one surrounding such should fear,

Or quake when in the presence of

People they know yet do not love.

Queer thoughts are these and thinking through

Return then to my thoughts of you;

So, tell me when in ancient time

The year that poets spoke in rhyme;

Unless you do not know, then please

Vent all your agonies on me

With words so mild, and as a child,

Xcessive should no poem be

Yet will I seek of poetry and seek therein the

Zion Tree.

## SUN-DAY

*I open my eyes and I see the sun;*

    *Such purity fills one with wonder*

        *This sun brings a welcome for everyone*

            *Dispersing the darkness asunder.*

*The sun is an image and metaphor*

    *Of Nature and rebirth and good;*

        *When anyone asks what the sun is for*

            *I'd say just one phrase if I could;*

        *For, suggesting that the Sun is GOOD*

            *I lose an 'O' and I see GOD.*

# FIGURES

There are 20 sheep in the field and I realise that

between them they have 80 legs

20 noses and 40 eyes;

if the farmer lets

one out there will be 19 sheep in the field;

and, if my maths is correct there will

be 19 noses and 38 eyes

blaring after sunrise;

as the lambs seek their mother's milk

and the world of nature will

continue for another round of days;

and I heard that 2000 care homes across the UK

has the Covid virus and that it was ok

for the health minister to simply say

we can do 25,000 tests today

when actually they have only done

14,000 yesterday.

The 25,000 are *people;*

the 14,000 are too few;

tomorrow the person missing out

on testing

might be *You*.

Figures are all around us;

they are used to confuse and confound us

but I still know that 20 sheep have 20 noses

and I am not confused yet.

When Captain Tom completed his 100 laps

he had raised 12 million pounds

for the NHS charity bank;

he made one promise

and kept it;

can you?

He has given us inspiration and hope that

"**Tom**orrow will be a good day."

## USE OF A SYMBOL

In my imaginative moments I drop thoughts on to empty pages,

arrange them like soldiers, sorting heights, lengths, vowels

and consonants, I put them in pairs and give them uniforms

with the use of drawing tools. I want to give them emphasis.

and insert an exclamation mark!

or two!!

and hope that will improve what has been written.

But the tutor is having none of it and derides

me for pretentious and over extensive use

of such symbols and I consign

the exclamation mark to the bin

!

# FREEDOM

The frog never meant to die;

He clung upon the driftwood of plants

Front legs embracing helplessly

Back legs hanging as one caught in the act

Of leaping.

When I pulled him out his eyes were dull;

10,000 tadpoles swam

Nibbling the plant as he leapt.

## PETRIFIED AND MOVING ON

From petrified moments grow survivors

To confound the mortuaries;

And furnaces which hourly blast our lives

Give ashen faces cause to spout a new regime;

From their gaping mouths and droughted eyes

Flow banners of tears;

Honouring those to whom honour is due;

Demanding in our springtime of rebirth

A world unfettered by false idols;

Love will come listening for answers;

Whatever faith we wear

We walk forward together;

And we will be dancing for joy;

Moving on;

God guiding us through;

Faith intact.

## THE SONG OF DAWN

Night's shadow loosed its pallid grip

as over the land a sigh slipped

out, reverberating from one

bound and now freed, and on one bough

 a tentative bird sound, such as

one would clear a throat, before

the tune, with melody profound

of flutes and pipes peeping,

tunefully cheeping like skylarks;

their wings swiftly fluttering

their song spewing and stuttering

and everywhere birdsong,

rioting in the blossom;

and in the hedges a chorus of blackbirds play,

while robin and thrush welcome the day.

## HOLDING BREATH IN AWE OF BEAUTY

*Moonlight shafted the conservatory roof*

*Slicing the floor into darkness and light;*

*Outside a hedgehog scurries, snout extended,*

*Invisible on the contours of the concrete path;*

*A quick gulp and I am confederate with nature;*

*Inhaling from its universal well;*

*A drumming like guns and carriages sound in the field beside me;*

*The deer herds are moving again;*

*Hooves become monsters of the night*

*Lithesome flanks glint and ghost among the grass;*

*They are a train passing;*

*They come from nowhere and are gone*

*Leaving an assault upon the senses;*

*A dying drumming, pulsing in the air;*

*You drape your frozen arms around your body*

*Pound the pimpled skin to keep it warm –*

*Until they have passed.*


*This night the world pooled your soul*

*And you acquiesced in the great oneness.*

## THE GREAT ESCAPE

Timmy the Tortoise eats leaves fresh and green;

One day he sought freedom like young Steve McQueen;

Off on a mission, to break from his cell

Well, a homely garden, that Timmy knows well.

This day Timmy spotted a hole in the fence

To make an escape route he'd need a few dents

He knocked with his shell and the rotten wood broke

Then out of the garden, oh, what a good joke -

The tortoise was running, he's wild and free;

Exiting the town on the A303.

Several hours passed before Timmy was missed

His 'Mum' began crying 'I can't believe this;

I've had little Timmy for 40 odd years

Forever he's lost; it's the worst of my fears.'

Her daughter said 'No, I will help sort this out,

I'll find you your Timmy, set posters about'.

She 'phoned up the vets and the rescue shops too

But Timmy's poor 'Mummy' was all in a stew.

Yet somewhere her Timmy was having great fun

Racing down highways and the 'A three eight one',

When daylight had ended the tortoise felt lost

With hundreds of junctions and dark roads to cross

Then Timmy was seen in the beam from some lights

A lady soon caught him and set him to rights,

He went to a Shelter and there he was found

Then taken to 'Mum' - where he was 'Grounded'!

## HECTOR COMES TO TEA

Hector the elephant was coming to tea;

He wanted cream cakes, cream scones and jam;

I said these cakes are much too sweet for me,

And wanted to give him brown bread and ham.

But Hector Henry Heuston as usual got his way,

( - to call him by his full and proper name!)

So I gave him five cream cakes wrapped up in hay,

And he ate them all down, just the same.

He swung his fluffy trunk upon the table,

And clambered his heavy legs upon the chair;

Then he scoffed the cakes as fast as he was able,

Which made his friends around him stare!

For never had they seen an elephant at tea

Who could eat five cream cakes mixed with hay,

Then fall from his chair, and Hrumph very loudly,

"Thanks, that's enough cream cake, even for me!"

## CAT NAP CHARADE

The charlatan cat with purr and drum

filled her throat with a lazy hum;

vibration running through her length

like a pulsing heart that sent

the favoured cat purring with contentment.

And for a while,

in the magical mind of her closed eyes

I embraced her feline smile

and realised with an inner mock at myself

it was all pretence,

and I wondered at her knowing

as if with some sixth feline sense

I thought her sleeping.

Then came a space of calm,

a coupling of serenity;

I stroking her coat in full knowledge

of my complicity,

when, like seeding dandelions, I found their puffing heads

were mirrored in her floating wisps of fur,

in spring time moult,

settling on my mouth, catching in my throat

like so many Fairy sticks clinging,

and joyously freed, as if drunk

at some bizarre ritual dance,

blessed by God, or left upon a pillow

still holding the curled warmth

of her body.

## LONGINGS

I am here, just longing to touch your hand;

Longing to feel the cool skin of cheek under my palm;

To caress you with my mother's love in my aching fingers;

Longing at the world's beginning and the moon's rising

To know you are here with my empty soul

That paints away the colours of the flowers you do not share

With me;

Longing to touch my family with my heart rather than my eyes alone;

To touch friends whose eyes alight with laughter and shared memories;

Unbounded hugs, kisses and eager chatter;

Real live chatter.

Imagine that.

To feel alive and live my life as an atom of theirs that I carry within me;

Longing for more than a photo;

Crying for more than a face on a screen which grieves

That when we see each other we are laughing with faces but our tears

Are unseen;

Welcome the tomorrow

When we will LIVE.

# WAR TIME POVERTY

The idle thimble belonged to Nell

Who laughed and played and never did anything well.

The little brass thimble behaved as it should

But poor little Nell she never did anything good.

Her struggling father and mother too

Knew poor little Nell would never have anything new.

The little brass thimble had work to do

But poor little Nell who laughed and played never knew.

## NOW YOU SEE IT, NOW YOU DON'T

The ice cream came, with a squawk of warning;

And a seagull or two, who were always hovering;

But the child had wanted a day at the sea

With an ice cream cone, or two, or three …

Then a flock of gulls flew overhead;

"Watch out, my dear," the seller said;

But the girl in pink with ribbons in her hair;

Waved her cone and didn't care;

She didn't see the gull as he rose

That pinched the cone from under her nose.

## IT'S CLEANING TIME

It's a solitary life in self isolation;

Staying at home, preserving the nation

For youngsters and children who don't even see -

The coronavirus is getting to me;

I'm filling my time with a round of spring cleaning

When I'd rather be running or trampolining;

I spend my days with my 'Marigolds' on

Hands in water and soap suds on -

Carpets and paintwork and windows and floors;

Mopping up stains and scrubbing down doors;

The washing machine is sharing my plight,

Washing by day and tumbling by night;

The brass bowl is polished, the silver pot too;

Everything smelling like lavender dew;

I'd rather be sharing my lovely clean house

With more than the cats and their little dead mouse;

I'm longing to invite some friends home for tea -

Or lunch, or dinner, or a simple coffee;

I want to stop cleaning! I want to shout 'Done!'

I want to start living, and having some FUN.

## HANKERIN' TO BE IDLE

The Spring cleaning's done so what can I do

To ease all this boredom? Aah, gardening will do;

So, I get out the shears, the hoe and the spade

And some big fluffy gloves, then flop in the shade -

In deep concentration about what I can do

To *avoid* the hoeing – 'Oh, I'll leave it to you,'

I say to my husband, who really is keen

To prove his prowess with the mowing machine;

He pushes the mower out front and out back,

I tell him he's clever and he has the knack

Of keeping all tidy, and I'm oh so impressed –

With watching him do it.  Now I need a rest.

I look at the flowers, the weeds and the clover

I watch them for hours and never get over

The thrill that it gives me to see a job done

By somebody else – while I'm having fun;

The virus is with us and Time's on my side

So, I get on the mower and go for a ride.

# HAIKU

(1)

His claw catches me

Purr-filled song scagging my heart

Awesome memories

(2)

The rose that is blown;

It's beauty no longer there.

Yet love comes again.

# WOOLLEN LIFE

Spring sun; the sheep begin to pant
      Heavy, laden with pounds of waxen wool
           And shearing day is coming.
Young life, and youthful lambs do play
      Heady, joyous like kids racing in school
           The days are getting shorter.

## FUTURE DREAR

It's a gloomy day

when the grass is gone

and the lambs all go away

for sound is gone

and the baa-ing nights of misplaced 'mums'

are replaced by deepened silence.

Except the singing trees

accompanies the blue tits

and the wanton thrills of songthrush

come spilling through falling rain

with the wondrous flute of the blackbird.

Later there will be a welcome day

when the grass has greened

and grown

and sheep and lambs return

and I will delight that they are home.

# LOST

Floundering in mud on a winter's day

Black clouds approaching

Shredded with pinking shears

Into dirty tails scarring the barren moors;

The coming night was pregnant with coldness;

Biting winds wrapped up the gorse and heather

Into the blackening coombs

It was a bad night for floundering.

Somewhere a lantern shone for everyone.

## THE VITAL DIFFERENCE

A buzzard soars above sun struck gorse

past the dark wood, blowing its coarse

high pitched mew into the hot spring

day and another joins it and soaring

together they begin swooping over

fields dotted with celandine, daisies and clover

and dandelion; and the buzzards are on duty,

majestic, alert, full of beauty and determination,

looping in huge circles in any combination

so long as they find food, more food and I see a rambling

group of lambs scampering across the stretch of sand

and dry dirt that they had made over the days

 since first entering the field, and I see the way

it appears to be an airstrip for a bi-plane;

something that could have been made

as a hasty creation for the war, but the bevy of lambs

careering and by now numbering a dozen, strong

limbed and round bellied, suddenly stops,

mid jump, and begin banging their heads

together, springing back, flip kicking

out, bounding upon the grass;

one butting a woolly pass

at another, which jumps and

springs away, then racing began

again as I watch from the window;

while the tv screen flashes with

the latest death toll

and I know,

in spite of everything, it is ok

being at home; the birds

and the animals

are living

in freedom.


and I am alive.

## COVID 2020

At some future stage when we have plenty

To do, we will ask "What did we do in 2020?"

We will look for photos of things which we did

Completely forgetting isolation and Covid

19, which sounds very much like something the Americans

Knew in Vietnam, or we might think of Michigan

State, and the crisis that cut off lives in New York

For a long time, and only ended through work

And sacrifice, at some future date, by a few, for the nation;

So that we could all be safe in self isolation

Which seems to be the only activity which we

Can all undertake, in an act of selfless individuality

And which, though it was difficult to do

For a time, we all came to love those in the 'Blue'

Of the NHS and the caring services, who never

Thought of themselves or their safety, or whatever;

And every day putting themselves in more danger

Than any of us, on behalf of a stranger;

Someone of whom they never even knew the name

Of, and as we know, all the same

Can be said of the whole caring profession,

And now, here is a governmental confession

Of shame, because these 'saints', these workers of charity

Are paid a fraction of those in the entertainment industry.

Bless the cleaners, and the drivers, all earning a very small wage

Though their importance to us is not broadcast on stage;

Where are our values, I put it to you?

Where are the morals of the rich, for the few? *


*Not all in this bracket can be tarred with this brush- but shame on those who can.

# REDUNDANCIES

Handbags are redundant

and the people carrying them are saving money

whilst the people selling the handbags

and things to go in them are in agony

because everything that was so important

has become redundant, and

we have made ourselves slaves

to the world of retail therapy

not knowing any longer

if we really need the stuff,

or simply enjoy buying the 'stuff',

and after its purchase the item

is immediately redundant

because we have usually already got one,

or two, or more at home, and then

we have to sort things out to make room

for the new (if we still like it, of course),

but at least we're keeping the 'bin men'

happy and at least we know that they

won't be redundant,

in fact, by keeping our handbags employed

we can keep the bin men employed,

oh, and the charity shops -

since most of our clothes purchases will end up

there in their myriad of bags

with new and used tags –

that just goes to show how much we really needed,

or simply did not need, the clothes

which we have purchased

at a discounted price and because it looks

so good on the hanger, but when we get it home

it doesn't look so good any more,

and what did I buy it for, but look

how much I saved, and it is really an art

how the marketing people of the shops

can wheedle the money from our handbags

when we don't even know what they are doing,

yet we always suspect them,

and you would expect that if

we suspected them we might do something

about it, but we don't

because we enjoy the experience

of taking our handbags to the shops

and getting out the credit and debit

cards that has made purchasing so much easier,

and I am starting to feel sorry

for the credit cards now, because suddenly

they are redundant too and I wonder

what the world is coming to when we have time

to look out of our windows because we are no longer

going out shopping,

and we can hear bird song!

## WHEN THIS VIRUS IS OVER

I'm going to dress up and sit for hours in a coffee

Shop and eat too much cake, and buy toffee

In the largest confectioner's tin

I can find, and then I will ring

The dentist and say I'm right sorry that

All this self isolation and self denial might

Be good for a family of dormice

But that it's really not so nice

For the likes of me who wants to be

Social and visit the shops and the sea

Side and make castles in the sand

And pat stranger's dogs with my hand

Without worrying if the virus is on

Its collar, or lead, or long

To be more than two metres away

From their owner and so stray

To the other side of the path

With a false exclamation and a laugh

Which doesn't quite reach the eyes

Because you might, much to your surprise

Catch something, take home something which

You don't know about until your throat itch

And you cough and your temperature rise

And you suddenly realise

That you might have, just might have

Not really knowing if you do have

Since there are no tests available

To check if you have, if you are able

To have the virus!

Aaattchoo!!  Well bless us

Everyone.

## VE CELEBRATIONS

Let this be remembered as a good day for our nation

As we acknowledge the Forces of the victory celebration

In Europe, seventy-five years ago,

Yet we are left baffled and wondering,

As they did when Doodlebugs were thundering

And destroying their cities below

Where is God in all of this?


This day marks a surrender, and a riotous jubilation

In cities and towns, and factories across the nation

And in farmhouses when everyone cheered

Because the saviours of our race were coming home

From Norway and Egypt, Moscow and Rome

Where more had been lost than anyone feared,

And everyone asked, where is God in all of this?


Yet the churches were working, and during the war

Fine firemen were protecting St Paul's steeple, before

The fires could destroy it since it was a sign of hope;

But Time has moved on and the people we hear cheering

And clapping on Thursdays are within the hearing

Of the NHS and carers, and all those who cope

With an impossible task, and we ask Where is God in all of this?

Well, where is God in all of this, come Hail Triumphant Holy Day

Welcome victory, and the 7$^{th}$ of May?

The circle has turned and we have a different kind of war

We are still a nation cheering for the people

Though no one is protecting St Paul's steeple

Because a sign hangs on the cathedral door

'SORRY WE ARE CLOSED'. So, where is God in all of this?


Can He still be in the air that I breathe?

Well, today, He is on the internet and, I believe.

As people return to greater kindness

Towards their neighbour, there is just a chance

He might survive, and Nature will return to this world of silence

In our fields and forests and trees; making much less

Reason to ask, 'Where is God in all of this?'


Our world has turned its seventy-five year

Circle, and there will be many hardships I fear

Up ahead, as there were after the war

But let us enjoy this time of peaceful recreation

Let us live more kindly and with less condemnation

Let us build up our country, as our parents did before

And remember, as always, God is with us.

## WHAT CAN YOU DO NOW?

These poems were written in response to the loss of a beloved brother in law, who was greatly supported by the Marie Curie staff, and whose funeral was not able to go ahead due to the Covid 19 restrictions in force at that time. I began writing A Poem A Day as my challenge to raise funds for Marie Curie, and wrote a total of 31 poems, the last one being written on $7^{th}$ May when a COBR meeting was due to discuss the lifting of some restrictions.

If you have enjoyed reading these poems and would like to help me raise funds for Marie Curie, you can go to my justgiving page and make a donation. Any contribution would make a difference to the many families who use the Marie Curie charity. The message is very easy – if you help them, they can help you. Thank you, and God bless you.

**Justgiving.com/fundraising/fran-bridger**

**Thank you for reading these poems.**

# A POEM A DAY